HEALTHY DIGESTION, HEALTHY BODY

Faulty digestion is directly responsible for a vast array of illnesses—everything from heartburn and constipation to ulcers. But studies show that many widespread illnesses—for example, arthritis, asthma, chronic fatigue syndrome, food allergies and sensitivities, migraine headaches and psoriasis—are indirectly caused by leaky gut syndrome. This book provides a comprehensive guide to the condition, ways to test for it and to detoxify your body, as well as dozens of nutritional and herbal self-care ideas so you can restore your digestive function to optimal health.

ABOUT THE AUTHOR

Elizabeth Lipski, M.S., C.C.N. is a clinical nutritionist who has worked in the field of nutrition and holistic health since receiving her master's degree in 1979. In 1991 she became board certified by the Clinical Nutrition Certification Board. Lipski was formerly president of the California chapter and on the national board of the International & American Associations of Clinical Nutritionists, editorial board of the *Journal of Applied Nutrition* and the advisory board of the American Academy of Nutrition and Preventive Medicine.

She is currently in private practice and divides her time among clinical work, telephone consultations, teaching and lecturing. She lives on the island of Kauai with her husband and two sons.

For information about her services, call: 808-826-2562; fax: 808-826-4559; or e-mail: lipski@aloha.net.

Leaky Gut Syndrome

What to do about a health threat
that can cause arthritis, allergies
and a host of other illnesses.

Elizabeth Lipski, M.S., C.C.N.

KEATS PUBLISHING

LOS ANGELES

NTC/Contemporary Publishing Group

Acknowledgments

I want to thank the following people for sharing their expertise with me: Eleanor Barrager, R.D., Trent Nichols, M.D., Corey Resnick, N.D. and Ray Rosenthal, M.D. Also thanks to Stephen Barrie and Marty Lee for allowing me to use previously published illustrations and materials. Also to Susan Davis, my fearless editor who tamed my thoughts.

Also special thanks to my family who persevered through another writing project. Thanks to my husband, Stephen, who provided the needed space in his busy schedule so that I could focus on this project. Thanks to Kyle for being so willing to make dinner several times a week. And thanks to Arthur for helping with cooking and cleaning chores.

Leaky Gut Syndrome is intended solely for informational and educational purposes, and not as medical advice. Please consult a health professional if you have questions about your health.

Contents

INTRODUCTION

I know *leaky gut syndrome* sounds weird, but if you'll bear with me, I promise you'll find the topic one of nearly universal interest. Lots of us have a leaky gut and don't even know it. If you have such common complaints as arthritis, asthma, an autoimmune disease, digestive problems, fatigue, food allergies or sensitivities, you probably have a leaky gut.

The digestive system plays an important role in total body health that was never understood before as clearly as it is today. Each year we find out more about how our digestive system looks out for us, protecting us from microbes and toxic substances. It plays an enormous role in our immune system, providing the first line of defense. It acts as a barrier that decides what to let into our bloodstream and what to keep out. Unfortunately, in today's fast-paced world, the health of the digestive tract often becomes compromised, leading to poor health. If food is not properly digested, cells don't receive the nourishment they need for proper functioning.

This book provides you with a step-by-step plan for recognizing, understanding and treating leaky gut syndrome. The approach is from a biological rather than a medical viewpoint—looking for root causes of *dis-ease* and *dis-comfort*. It's impossible to discuss leaky gut syndrome without also discussing the important detoxification function of the liver, intestinal flora and microbial balance in the digestive system. These systems work together to keep our immune system healthy, which keeps us healthy. When these systems become overburdened, we feel it.

The solutions presented require your personal involvement in your own well-being. You will find out about new lab tests that can help diagnose your problems and monitor your treatment. You'll find information about cleansing, feeding and nurturing your body and soul—simple, effective tools to improve the way you feel. Healing leaky gut syndrome can help you treat the underlying cause or contributing factor to your illness and symptoms. Without addressing gut permeability as an issue, many people will never maintain the vibrancy and vitality they deserve. Come with me on a journey towards wellness.

LEAKY GUT SYNDROME: WHAT IS IT?

Leaky gut syndrome is really a nickname for the more formal term *increased intestinal permeability*, which underlies an enormous variety of illnesses and symptoms. It's not a disease or an illness itself. Rather, it manifests itself in an enormous variety of ways depending on your genes and your personal ecology. You wouldn't think that AIDS, allergies, ankylosing spondylitis, arthritis, asthma, autoimmune illnesses, celiac disease, chronic hepatitis, Crohn's disease, cystic acne, eczema, fatigue, inflammatory bowel disease, migraines, multiple-chemical sensitivities, psoriasis, Reiter's syndrome, rheumatoid arthritis, schizophrenia and Sjogren's syndrome would have anything in common, but they do.[1] People who have any of these conditions usually also have a leaky gut. The list of health conditions associated with increased intestinal permeability grows each year as we gain further understanding of the role the gut plays in the immune system and central nervous system. Depending on our own susceptibilities, we may develop a wide variety of signs, symptoms and health problems. Leaky gut syndrome is associated with the following medical problems or conditions.

Common Clinical Conditions Associated with Increased Intestinal Permeability[2]

Acne	HIV positive
Aging	Hives
AIDS	Inflammatory bowel disease
Alcoholism	Intestinal infections
Allergic disorders	Irritable bowel syndrome
Ankylosing spondylitis	Liver dysfunction
Arthritis/inflammatory joint disease	Malabsorption
Asthma	Malnutrition
Autism	Multiple chemical sensitivities
Celiac disease	NSAID enteropathy
Chemotherapy	Pancreatic insufficiency
Childhood hyperactivity	Psoriasis
Chronic fatigue syndrome	Reiter's syndrome
Crohn's disease	Rheumatoid arthritis
Cystic fibrosis	Schizophrenia
Eczema	Systemic lupus erythematosus
Endotoxemia	Thermal injury
Environmental illness	Trauma
Food allergies or sensitivities	Ulcerative colitis
Giardiasis	

In addition to these clinical conditions, people with leaky gut syndrome display a wide variety of symptoms.

Symptoms Associated with Leaky Gut Syndrome[3]

Abdominal pain	Gas
Aggressive behavior	Indigestion
Anxiety	Mood swings
Asthma	Nervousness
Bed wetting	Poor exercise tolerance
Bloating	Poor immunity
Chronic joint pain	Poor memory
Chronic muscle pain	Primary biliary cirrhosis
Confusion	Recurrent bladder infections
Constipation	Recurrent vaginal infections
Diarrhea	Shortness of breath
Fatigue and malaise	Skin rashes
Fevers of unknown origin	Toxic feelings
Fuzzy thinking	

The conditions in the chart can arise from a variety of causes, but leaky gut syndrome may underlie more classic diagnoses. If you have any of the common symptoms or disorders associated with leaky gut syndrome, ask your physician to order an intestinal permeability test to see if that is contributing to your problem (see page 27).

HOW DIGESTION WORKS

Our digestive system provides us with our most intimate contact with our environment. Our digestive tract is a 25- to 35-foot hose that runs from mouth to anus. Its function is to turn the foods we eat into microscopic particles that the cells can use for energy, maintenance and repair. It has as many nerve endings as the spine and plays an important role in immune function. The intestinal tract provides a barrier between the outside world and what actually gets absorbed into us, becoming our bodies. If spread flat, our digestive system would cover an area the size of a tennis court. It repairs and replaces itself every three to five days.

The sloughed-off material contains enzymes and fluids which are recycled to help the digestive function. Because of its large surface area and its constant exposure to foods, microbes, irritants and toxins, it forms a first line of defense for our immune system function. If the intestinal barrier is breached, microbes and foreign substances gain entrance into us and can create nearly any sort of trouble imaginable.

The saying "you are what you eat" is primarily true. From birth to death, we continually create and recreate ourselves from the nourishment we put inside our bodies. Nutritious foods are the right place to start on the path to digestive wellness. But many people eat all the "right" foods and still have digestive problems. You must be able to digest foods by breaking them into tiny particles, absorb the resulting food mash through the intestinal lining and into the blood-stream, bring nutrients into the cells (assimilation) and eliminate waste products through the kidneys and bowels. Health can and does break down at any of these places. Leaky gut syndrome is primarily an absorption problem—too many substances are allowed to pass from the intestinal lining into the bloodstream.

UNDERSTANDING THE SMALL INTESTINE

Let's take a look at the small intestine, which is hardly small! If uncoiled, it would average 15 to 20 feet in length. It has a paradoxical function: to let nutrients into our blood-stream while blocking the absorption of large molecules, microbes and toxins. This barrier consists of a single layer, about the thickness of an eyelid. Alcohol, foods, medications and stress can cause the intestinal lining to become compromised. These substances irritate and inflame the intestinal lining, causing tiny tears. The intestinal lining loses its ability to act properly as a filter and leaks, hence the name "leaky gut syndrome."

The process of digestion is finished in the small intestine, and food substances begin to get absorbed into our blood-stream for use by individual cells. In essence we eat to nourish each and every one of those itty-bitty cells. If they don't have a consistent supply of nutrients, they can't function properly. What goes on at a micro level manifests itself on a system level: we don't feel so hot!

Nutrients are absorbed through hundreds of small finger-like folds, called *villi*, in the intestinal wall, which, in turn, are covered by millions of microvilli. (Think of them as small loops on a velvety towel, which have smaller threads projecting from them.) The villi and microvilli are covered with mucus and bacteria which protect the tissue. Though only one layer thick, the villi and microvilli perform multiple functions of producing digestive enzymes, absorbing nutrients and blocking absorption of substances that aren't useful to the body. This surface is often called the *brush border* because the villi and microvilli look like bristles on a brush under a microscope.

A healthy intestinal lining allows only properly digested fats, proteins and starches to pass through so they can be assimilated. At the same time it also provides a barrier to keep out large undigested molecules, bacterial products and foreign substances. This is called the *barrier function* of the

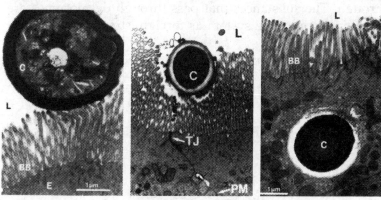

Healthy brush borders produce digestive enzymes, absorb nutrients and block absorption of foreign substances. Damaged brush borders (shown here) allow antigenic substances into the bloodstream. (Illustrations provided by Great Smokies Diagnostic Laboratory)

gastrointestinal mucosal lining. The intestinal lining lets substances move across the barrier in two main ways—either through the cell itself or between cells. Most nutrients pass through the cell itself by either *diffusion* or *active transport.* Diffusion is a simple process which equalizes the concentrations of substances inside and outside the cells, much the same way that salt in a glass of water spreads evenly throughout the water. Chloride, free fatty acids, magnesium, potassium and sodium move into the cells by diffusion. Most nutrients are moved through the brush borders via active transport. Carrier molecules transport nutrients like molecular taxi cabs. Amino acids, fatty acids, glucose, minerals and vitamins cross cell membranes with the help of these taxis, which allows for greater concentration of a substance than simple diffusion does.

In-between cells are junctions called *desmosomes.* Normally, desmosomes form tight junctions and do not permit large molecules to pass through. But when an area is irritated and inflamed, these junctions loosen up, allowing larger molecules to pass. When the intestinal lining is further damaged, even larger substances of particle size are allowed through. The substances that pass through desmosomes are seen by our immune system as foreign, stimulating an antibody reaction.

When the intestinal lining is damaged even more, sub-

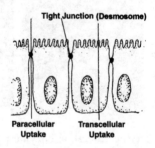

Desmosomes should always form tight junctions. When inflamed or irritated, the junctions loosen, allowing substances to pass through.

stances larger than particle size—disease-causing bacteria and fungus, potentially toxic molecules and undigested food particles—are allowed to pass directly through the weakened cell membranes. They go directly into the bloodstream, activating antibodies and alarm substances called *cytokines*. The cytokines alert our lymphocytes (white blood cells) to battle the particles. Oxidants are produced in this battle, causing further irritation and inflammation far from the digestive system. (See the section on Getting Well under antioxidants below.)

The digestive tract is normally coated with a mucus layer which not only keeps foreign substances out but has a direct immunological function. This mucus layer, and skin and mucus secretions throughout the body, is filled with an antibody called *secretory IgA*. Secretory IgA (sIgA) provides a line of defense against bacteria, food residue, fungus, parasites and viruses. It neutralizes invaders and prevents them from attaching to membranes. Deficiency of secretory IgA is the most common immunodeficiency. Low levels make us more susceptible to infection and may be a fundamental cause of asthma, autoimmune disease, candidiasis, celiac disease, food allergies and more. A study of people with Crohn's disease or ulcerative colitis found that all of them had low levels of sIgA.[4] High levels of sIgA are found in people whose immune systems are overloaded, as in chronic fatigue syndrome and HIV.

Seventy percent of our immune system is located in or around the digestive system.[5] Called *gut-associated lymphatic tissues* (GALT), it's located in the lining of the digestive tract and in the intestinal mucus. If our digestive system is presented with a foreign substance, an antigen, specialized cells called *M-cells* carry the antigen to the lining of the digestive tract. There they are "checked out" (sampled) by specialized cells called *Peyer's patches* in the intestinal lining. They, in turn, alert B and T cells to begin processing the antigens. They carry them back to the intestinal mucosa where they are gobbled up by macrophages. Secretory IgA, which are also on constant alert for foreign substances, are also in the gut mucosa. Their arousal signals cytokines to begin the inflammatory process designed to rid our bodies of antigenic materials.

HOW LEAKY GUT SYNDROME DEVELOPS

The mucus layer is weakened, allowing bacteria and fungi to pass into the bloodstream and throughout the body. When intestinal bacteria wander from the intestine and colonize in other parts of the body, we call it *bacterial translocation*. This can occur if there is a disruption of the balance of the normal gut flora which results in bacterial overgrowth or decreased immune resistance. Physical disruption, for example, after surgery or tube feeding in hospitals, can also cause bacterial translocation.[6] (It has been strongly suggested that this bacterial translocation, when coupled with leaky gut syndrome, plays a role in multiple organ failure.[7]) It is often found in people with leaky gut syndrome. For example, *Blastocystis hominis*, a bacteria which can causes GI problems, has been found in the synovial fluid of people with arthritis.

UNDERSTANDING THE CONNECTION BETWEEN THE LIVER AND THE GUT

It is impossible to discuss leaky gut syndrome without also discussing the role of the liver in detoxification. The liver is the organ primarily responsible for converting toxic or harmful substances into safe byproducts that can be easily excreted. The liver also has numerous other functions, including maintenance of blood sugar levels; producing cholesterol, triglycerides and bile; breaking down unneeded hormones; and manufacturing thousands of compounds to detoxify our bodies.

The liver acts as a filter for nearly everything that enters our bloodstream and changes toxic substances by converting them into a form that our bowels and kidneys can excrete. It does this in a two-stage process. Phase one is an enzymatic process called the *cytochrome P450 pathway*. Many toxic substances are fat soluble, so the enzymes in this pathway make the toxins more soluble so they can be eliminated effectively. If not eliminated, they are stored in the liver and throughout the body. Phase two converts these substances to a water-soluble form so they can be excreted in the urine and stool. These processes require specific nutrients in order to work correctly. (Liver detoxification pathways can be measured by a test called the liver detoxification profile, which is described below.)

Leaky gut syndrome puts an extra burden on the liver because it allows extra toxins to circulate through the bloodstream. And when the liver is bombarded by inflammatory irritants from incomplete digestion, it has less energy to neutralize chemical substances. When overwhelmed, it stores these toxins in fat cells, much the same way that we put boxes in the garage or basement to deal with later. If the liver has time later, it can deal with the stored toxins, but most commonly it is busy dealing with what is newly coming in and never catches up. As these toxins mount up, they are a continued source of inflammation in the body.

Our livers today are so bombarded with substances to break down that they cannot completely do their job. Leaky gut, along with alcohol, environmental pollutants, toxic chemicals from food and toxic byproducts of our own metabolism, overloads the liver and increases the risk of free radical damage throughout the body. Therefore, it is essential to help the liver in every way possible to reduce the total body load of toxins so that it can work efficiently and effectively.

Do You Have Leaky Gut Syndrome?

The following leaky gut syndrome questionnaire[8] doesn't provide a definitive diagnosis, but it can help you assess the functioning of your small intestine. It is not intended to replace a physician's care or an intestinal permeability test. However, if you score high on this self-test, seek a physician who is knowledgeable about leaky gut to help you.

0 = Symptom is not present or rarely present
1 = Mild/sometimes
2 = Moderate/often
3 = Severe/almost always

INTESTINAL PERMEABILITY/LEAKY GUT SYNDROME, DYSBIOSIS

Constipation and/or diarrhea	0	1	2	3
Abdominal pain or bloating	0	1	2	3
Mucus or blood in stool	0	1	2	3
Joint pain or swelling, arthritis	0	1	2	3
Chronic or frequent fatigue or tiredness	0	1	2	3
Food allergies, sensitivities or intolerance	0	1	2	3
Sinus or nasal congestion	0	1	2	3
Chronic or frequent inflammations	0	1	2	3
Eczema, skin rashes or hives (urticaria)	0	1	2	3
Asthma, hayfever or airborne allergies	0	1	2	3
Confusion, poor memory or mood swings	0	1	2	3
Use of nonsteroidal antiinflammatory drugs (aspirin, Tylenol, Motrin)	0	1	2	3
History of antibiotic use	0	1	2	3
Alcohol consumption or alcohol makes you feel sick	0	1	2	3
Ulcerative colitis, Crohn's disease or celiac disease	0	1	2	3
Total:				

Score 1-5: Leaky gut less apt to be present.
Score 6-10: Leaky gut may possibly be present.
Score 7-19: Leaky gut probably present.
Score 20+: Leaky gut almost certainly present.

There is no single cause of leaky gut syndrome, but some of the most common are listed below.[9] Then we'll discuss some of them one at a time in order of importance.

Causes of Increased Intestinal Permeability

Prolonged use of nonsteroidal anti-inflammatory drugs (NSAIDs)
Chronic stress
Dysbiosis (defined in text)
Environmental contamination/toxic substances
Aging
Food allergies and sensitivities
Endotoxins
Chemotherapy/radiation therapy

AIDS
Gastrointestinal disease
Immune overload
Deficiency of secretory IgA
Overuse of alcoholic beverages
Trauma
Chronic infections/presence of pathogenic bacteria, parasites and yeast

PAIN MEDICATIONS

Nonsteroidal anti-inflammatory drugs (NSAIDS) like aspirin, ibuprofen and indomethacin are a common cause of leaky gut syndrome. NSAIDs work by blocking prostaglandins, which are tiny messengers that circulate throughout the body. Some prostaglandins cause healing and repair; others cause pain and inflammation. However, NSAID drugs block *all* prostaglandins. The pain may be gone, but the healing process is blocked. Since the digestive tract repairs and replaces itself every three to five days, prolonged use of NSAIDs blocks its repair. GI side effects are well known: the lining becomes weak, inflamed and leaky, causing leaky gut syndrome. NSAID use also increases the risk of ulcers of the stomach and duodenum. These drugs also cause bleeding, damage to the mucus membranes of the intestines and GI inflammation. NSAIDs can lead to colitis and relapses of ulcerative colitis. In fact, I have a client who had ulcerative colitis ten years ago. His disease appeared to be in total remission for a full decade, but when he began taking NSAIDs for pain, it flared up severely. Even moderate use of NSAIDs has been shown to increase gut permeability.

DYSBIOSIS

The term "dysbiosis" was coined by Dr. Eli Metchnikoff, a scientist who was awarded the Nobel prize in 1908 for his work on friendly bacterial flora. Normally, we have hundreds of types of bacteria living inside our digestive tract. In fact, we have more bacteria in our digestive tract than cells in our body. Many of these are helpful (flora), some are neutral (commensal) and others are harmful (pathogenic). A disordered balance of these microbes is called "dysbiosis," which comes from "symbiosis," meaning living together in mutual harmony, and "dys," which means *not*.

Dr. Metchnikoff found that the bacteria in yogurt prevented and reversed bacterial infection. (He named it *Lactobacillus bulgaricus* after the long-living, yogurt-loving peasants in Bulgaria.) His research proved that lactobacilli could displace many disease-producing organisms and reduce the toxins they generated. He believed these endotoxins, which are toxins produced from substances inside the body, shortened the lifespan. In the 1940s he advocated use of lactobacilli for ptomaine poisoning, which became widely used in Europe. In recent decades Metchnikoff's work has taken a back seat to modern therapies like antibiotics and immunization programs, which scientists hoped would conquer infectious diseases.

However, new lab tests and research have revitalized interest in this area. We are finding many microbes that don't really belong in the digestive tract. The unbalanced microbes often form chemicals that are poisonous to the cells around them and to the person they live in. A wide variety of substances are produced, including amines, ammonia, hydrogen sulfide, indoles, phenols and secondary bile acids.[10] These substances may hurt the intestinal lining directly by damaging the brush borders and become absorbed into the bloodstream, causing systemwide effects. Unlike salmonella bacteria, which cause immediate food-poisoning reactions, the microbes which cause dysbiosis are generally low-virulence organisms. They cause chronic problems which go undiagnosed, becoming deep-seated in the great majority of cases.

The most common cause of dysbiosis is use of prescription and over-the-counter medications. Antibiotics, for instance, change the balance of intestinal microbes. They simultaneously kill both harmful and helpful bacteria throughout our digestive system, mouth, vagina and skin, leaving the territory to bacteria, parasites, viruses and fungi that are unaffected by the antibiotic. Most people can recover fairly easily from a single round of antibiotics, but even those with strong constitutions have trouble regaining their balance from repeated use of antibiotic drugs.

Published research has listed dysbiosis as a contributing cause in rheumatoid arthritis, autoimmune illness, B12 deficiency, chronic fatigue, cystic acne, the early stages of colon and breast cancer, eczema, food allergy/sensitivity, inflammatory bowel disease, irritable bowel syndrome, multiple sclerosis, psoriasis, Sjogren's syndrome and steatorrhea. These problems were previously unrecognized as having a microbial component.

ANTIBIOTICS

Antibiotics change the balance of intestinal microbes. Not terribly specific, antibiotics simultaneously kill both harmful and helpful bacteria, leaving the territory open to resistant bacteria, parasites, viruses and fungi. In a healthy gut these are kept in check by helpful microbes. When left unchecked, they colonize the area, contributing to inflammation, irritation and disease. Candida, a fungus, is the most common microbe to flourish in this new environment.

CANDIDA

The most prevalent and well-known type of dysbiosis is candidiasis, a fungal infection. Candida is found in nearly everyone and is compatible with good health in small amounts. Candida is usually controlled by friendly flora, our immune defense system and intestinal pH. If allowed to proliferate, however, it dominates areas of the digestive tract, causing havoc throughout the body. Candida fungi produce a chemical, called *acid protease*, which cleaves secretory IgA from the mucus membranes. This allows candida to anchor into and colonize on the mucus membranes. Once there the candida secrete toxins that are absorbed into the bloodstream and affect our immune system, hormone balance and thought processes. Candida are like bullies that push their way into the intestinal lining, destroying cells and brush borders. This damage allows macromolecules of partially digested food to pass through the lining. The macromolecules are the perfect size for antibodies to respond to. Your immune system then goes on alert for these specific foods so the next time you eat them, your antibodies will be waiting! The net result is increased sensitivity to foods and other food substances and the environment.

For example, a strong link exists between *Candida albicans* and asthma. Studies have found a reaction antibody to candida in 53 to 66 percent of all asthmatics tested.[11] This may be a result of steroid medication, which is well known to stimulate candida growth, but it may also be due to a deficiency of secretory IgA found in mucus membranes throughout the body as a consequence of asthma.[12]

Candida infections are usually triggered by use of antibiotics, birth control pills, steroid medications and alcoholic beverages, which contain substances that are toxic to our cells. Alcohol is metabolized in the liver where the toxins are either broken down or stored by the body. While alcoholic drinks contain few nutrients, they take many nutrients to metabolize. They are particularly good at gobbling up B-complex vitamins. Therefore, alcohol puts a strain on the liver, which affects digestive competency, and also damages the intestinal lining.

The most common symptoms of candida infections are abdominal bloating, anxiety, constipation, diarrhea (or both), depression, environmental sensitivities, fatigue, feeling worse on damp or muggy days or in moldy places, food sensitivities, fuzzy thinking, insomnia, low blood sugar, mood swings, premenstrual syndrome, recurring vaginal or bladder infections, ringing in the ears and sensitivities to perfume, cigarettes or fabric odors. Although these symptoms are the most prevalent, candida can masquerade in a diverse set of health problems.

Case Study: Virginia

Virginia came to see me in January 1996. Her main complaint was hemorrhoids. They bothered her so much she sat on an inflated donut-shaped tube most of the time. Her discomfort and itching during the night caused insomnia. In addition, she had rashes that occurred sporadically under her arms, breasts, in her pubic area and on the roof of her mouth. Virginia complained of lifelong irritable bowel syndrome, with alternating constipation and diarrhea and spasms. In addition to low energy and much fatigue, waking up each morning exhausted, she had dry skin, heavy menstrual cycles and was never really hungry. Two years after being a competitive triathlete with a weight of 130, she was forty pounds heavier, despite a lack of appetite.

Virginia scored very high on William Crook's candida questionnaire, so we asked her physician to do food allergy and sensitivity bloodwork while she went on an antifungal program. She changed her eating to high protein foods, with lots of fresh vegetables, potatoes, yams, brown rice and some oils. She avoided all fruit, sugar, grains except rice, vinegar, alcohol and dairy, except yogurt. We also had her take supplements of acidophilus and bifidobacteria, plus one with biotin, capryllic acid and garlic.

Virginia responded almost immediately. She began to sleep through the night without itching and wake up refreshed. Her diarrhea vanished, and as long as her fiber content was high, she experienced no further constipation. Her hemorrhoids healed completely. Her rashes disappeared, and from day two she had no colon spasms. Her appetite returned within two weeks; yet she began to consistently lose weight. Within three months, she had totally regained health and vitality in nearly every area.

Case Study: Mimi

Mimi initially came to me because she wanted to stop drinking alcohol. After her work day was completed, she'd sit down with a tumbler of liquor in front of the TV and drink until she passed out. She had previously quit drinking several times in programs and on her own. Three years previously, she developed asthma, for which she took three medications daily and used inhalers to stop attacks. However, she smoked two packs of cigarettes daily. In addition, Mimi had chronic vaginal yeast infections, mood swings and night blindness. Her favorite food was sausages, but she ate a wide variety of foods.

Mimi had read about a nutritional plan for alcoholics and wanted me to customize a program for her and provide support. During the next several months, Mimi had dramatic results. By going on a candida diet (described above) and a supplement program designed for her particular biochemistry, Mimi was able to stop drinking easily. Within two months her asthma had cleared, and with her doctor's approval she was able to discontinue all medication. Her night vision improved as well as her moods. She lost 25 pounds and her energy level doubled. One year later, she's feeling better than she's ever felt, and she has begun to tackle her cigarette smoking. Candida and nutritional deficiencies underlay her health problems.

STEROID MEDICATIONS

Steroid medications, like cortisone and prednisone, are two of the most effective emergency medicines available. They are used for a plethora of medical problems involving allergies, auto-immune illnesses and inflammation. Long-term use of these drugs depresses the immune system and can encourage growth of fungal infections in the GI tract and elsewhere in the body.

CANCER THERAPIES

Chemotherapy drugs and radiation therapy significantly disrupt GI balance and cause malabsorption of food and nutrients. Bacterial translocation has been well documented after radiation therapy. Radiation treatment of the mid-body can dramatically affect the intestinal lining, causing leaky gut.

CHRONIC STRESS

Prolonged stress changes the immune system's ability to respond quickly and affects our ability to heal. Our body reacts to these stressors by producing less secretory IgA and DHEA (an anti-aging, antistress adrenal hormone), slowing down digestion and peristalsis, reducing blood flow to digestive organs and producing toxic metabolites.

TOXIC OVERLOAD/ENVIRONMENTAL CONTAMINANTS

Daily exposure to hundreds of household and environmental chemicals and toxic metals overloads our immune defenses and causes delays of necessary routine repairs. Our immune system can only pay attention to so many places at one time. Parts of our body far away from the digestive system are affected. Connective tissue begins to break down, and we lose trace minerals like calcium, magnesium and potassium. Environmental chemicals deplete our reserve of buffering minerals, causing acidocis in the cells and swelling of tissues and cells. This is known as *leaky cells*—like having major internal plumbing problems!

POOR FOOD CHOICES

Poor food choices contribute to an imbalance of intestinal flora and pH. An intestinal tract that is too alkaline promotes dysbiosis. Low-fiber diets cause an increase in transit time, allowing toxic digestive byproducts to concentrate and irritate the gut mucosa. Processed foods invariably are low in nutrients and fiber and have high levels of food additives, sugar and restructured fats. These foods promote inflammation of the GI tract. In fact, even foods we normally think of as healthful can be irritating to the gut lining. For example, milk, an American staple, can be highly irritating to people with lactose intolerance.

FOOD AND ENVIRONMENTAL SENSITIVITIES

Food sensitivities and leaky gut exist in a chicken and egg relationship. Whether intestinal damage initiated the problem or foods irritated the intestines, they continue to multiply the damage. Eventually, people become more easily sensitized to food remnants while the gut becomes more and more inflamed.

True food allergies affect only a small percentage of the population, but food sensitivities are common. Food allergies, also called *type 1* or *immediate hypersensitivity reactions,* trigger reactions of type IgE antibodies which bind to the offending food antigens. The IgE reaction causes the release of cytokines and histamines, which results in closing of the throat, hives, itching, respiratory distress, runny nose, skin rashes and sometimes severe reactions of asthma and anaphylactic shock. These symptoms usually occur within minutes after the food is eaten. Physicians diagnose food allergies through the use of patch skin tests and RAST blood testing.

Food sensitivities, also called *delayed hypersensitivity reactions,* cause symptoms which are delayed, taking several hours to several days to appear. Long after you have eaten the offending food, symptoms occur. That makes tracking them down very difficult. Food sensitivities cause a wide number of symptoms typical of a leaky gut. Food particles enter the bloodstream through damaged mucosal membranes. The body recognizes them as foreign substances (antigens) and triggers an immune reaction. The liver also recognizes these antigens as toxins and begins breaking them down. Eating foods to which we are sensitive increases intestinal permeability, which, in turn, increases our propensity to develop more food sensitivities. It's a vicious cycle. Prolonged antibody response can overwhelm the liver's ability to eliminate these food antigens. Almost any food can cause a reaction, although the most common are wheat, beef, dairy products, eggs, pork and citrus fruits. These foods provoke 80 percent of food sensitivity reactions.

Symptoms Associated with Food & Environmental Sensitivities[13]

The following symptoms are related to many health conditions. Professional evaluation is needed to uncover the source of these symptoms and to establish if food sensitivities are involved.

Head: Chronic headaches, migraines, difficulty sleeping, dizziness

Mouth & Throat: Coughing, sore throat, hoarseness, swelling/pain, gagging, frequently clearing throat, sores on gums, lips and tongue

Eyes, Ears, Nose: Runny or stuffy nose, postnasal drip, ringing in ears, blurred vision, sinus problems, watery/itchy eyes, ear infections, hearing loss, sneezing attacks, hay fever, excessive mucus formation, dark circles under eyes, swollen, red or sticky eyelids

Heart & Lungs: Irregular heartbeat (palpitations, arrhythmia), asthma, rapid heartbeat, chest pain & congestion, bronchitis, shortness of breath, difficulty breathing

Gastrointestinal: Nausea and vomiting, constipation, diarrhea, irritable bowel syndrome, indigestion, bloating, passing gas, stomach pain, cramping, heartburn

Skin: Hives, skin rashes, psoriasis, eczema, dry skin, excessive sweating, acne, hair loss, irritation around eyes, rash

Muscle & Joint: General weakness, muscle/joint aches & pains, arthritis, swelling, stiffness

Energy & Activity: Fatigue, depression, mental dullness and memory lapses, difficulty getting your work done, apathy, hyperactivity, restlessness

Emotions & Mind: Mood swings, anxiety & tension, fear, nervousness, anger, irritability, aggressive behavior, binge eating or drinking, food cravings, depression, confusion, poor comprehension, poor concentration, difficulty learning

Overall: Overweight, underweight, fluid retention, dizziness, insomnia, genital itch, frequent urination

Additional Signs of Food Allergies in Children

In addition to the symptoms listed above, children with food sensitivities may have

Attention Deficit Disorder
Behavior problems
Learning problems
Reoccurring ear infections

Children with these problems will benefit from working with a nutritionally oriented health physician or clinical nutritionist.

Case Study: Timmy

Timmy, a 7-year-old first grader, had behavior problems. He had already been asked to leave one school, and it was likely that the private school he attended would ask him to leave at the end of the year. A pediatric neurologist concluded that he would benefit from taking Ritalin. Instead, his mother went to the library and found books on diet and behavior. On her own she removed dairy products, food additives and sugar from his diet. She contacted a local physician, and we worked as a team to help Timmy's behavior improve.

The minute Timmy walked into my office he asked me if he could drink some milk. This gave me an important clue because often the foods we crave most are the ones we are most sensitive to. Timmy lived on an egg and poultry farm and had allergies. When he caught colds, they developed into asthma.

I suggested that we run several tests and do an elimination/challenge diet. Timmy's blood test indicated that he was allergic to chicken and a few other foods in addition to dairy products. We removed them from his diet, continued his low-allergy diet and suggested a few nutritional supplements.

Within two weeks Timmy's teacher noticed that his behavior had improved without being notified that Timmy was doing anything different. Although Timmy subsequently got colds, he was no longer developing asthma, and his allergies generally improved. Timmy wasn't 100 percent better, but he found that he could control his emotions and behavior much more easily. Even at 7, he noticed the difference and found that he "liked himself better" this way. It wasn't easy giving up his favorite foods, but it was worth it to him!

DIAGNOSING LEAKY GUT SYNDROME AND OTHER DIGESTIVE PROBLEMS

Intestinal permeability testing can help you find out if you have leaky gut syndrome. A number of other tests are available to help you determine the underlying causes.

INTESTINAL PERMEABILITY TESTING

Testing for intestinal permeability is widely available and cost effective. The lactulose/mannitol test is the most commonly used. Mannitol and lactulose are water-soluble sugar molecules that our bodies cannot use or metabolize. They have differing sizes and weights and are absorbed into our bloodstream at different rates. Mannitol is easily absorbed into the cells by people with healthy digestion, whereas lactulose has such a large molecular size that it is only slightly absorbed. The test results of a person with healthy digestion show high levels of mannitol and low levels of lactulose. If large amounts of lactulose and mannitol are present, it indicates a leaky gut condition. If low levels of both sugars are found, it indicates general malabsorption of all nutrients. High lactulose levels with low mannitol levels have been found in people with celiac disease, Crohn's disease and ulcerative colitis.[14]

Any physician can order the test and give you a kit so you can do it at home and send it to a lab for analysis. First, you collect a random urine sample. Then, you drink a mannitol/lactulose solution and collect all your urine for 6 hours, which is sent to the laboratory. The resulting ratios of mannitol to lactulose are an indication of what is going on digestively. This test is often done in conjunction with a Comprehensive Digestive Stool Analysis (CDSA).

If your intestinal permeability test shows an increase in permeability, you may want to follow up with other lab tests that can help uncover underlying causes. Tests can determine if you have dysbiosis, food allergies, parasites and poor digestive function; a liver function profile may also be helpful.

COMPREHENSIVE DIGESTIVE STOOL ANALYSIS

Comprehensive digestive stool analysis (CDSA) is a test that checks for bacterial balance and health, digestive function and dysbiosis. If you have a positive intestinal permeability test, the CDSA may give you information about the underlying cause of your problem. The CDSA is used to determine what types of bacteria are present and measures beneficial, possibly harmful and disease-producing microbes. It also checks to see levels of candida. If present, cultures are made to see if they grow and what therapeutic agents will be most effective in eliminating them. In addition, the CDSA measures digestive function by determining how well a person can digest proteins, fats and carbohydrates, the level of cholecystekinin (pancreatic enzyme) and the amount of short-chain fatty acids and butyric acid in the colon. Some labs also include a dysbiosis index, which, based on the combined testing, gives a measure of normalcy or abnormalcy. Most labs run a sensitivity test and provide recommendations indicating how effective medications and natural remedies would be for that individual.

Case Study: Richard

Richard had ulcerative colitis characterized by bleeding with bowel movements, severe reactions to a large number of foods, rapid weight loss and fatigue. In partnership with his gastroenterologist, we ran a CDSA. The test showed that Richard had overgrowth of two dysbiotic bacteria (citrobacter and klebsiella) and *Candida parapsilosis*, a less common variety of candida. Because lab technicians actually culture the client's microbes to see what works most effectively to kill them, the patient's CDSA listed the medications to which the bacteria and fungi would respond to most effectively, which the physician prescribed. In addition, we set up a dietary regime that eliminated foods which were irritating his digestive system. With proper diet, supplementation and medication, Richard's bleeding stopped, he had normal bowel movements, he gained weight consistently, and he is no longer taking prednisone, which his physician had expected he would need for the rest of his life. The CDSA was validating to my client. He could finally "see" what was going on inside his body, which helped his self-esteem and his healing process tremendously. Because Richard has gotten so much better, he now has an optimistic view of his future health prospects and quality of life.

CANDIDA TESTING

Dr. William Crook has developed a questionnaire which helps determine if you have candidiasis. It is available in all of his books, as well as in my book, *Digestive Wellness*. It is also widely available from many health professionals who use complementary approaches. Many physicians also use CDSA or blood antibody testing to determine if candida is present.

PARASITOLOGY TESTING

Though we think of parasites as something we get from traveling in other countries, it's not true. According to the June 27, 1978, *Miami Herald*, the Centers for Disease Control (CDC) in Atlanta found that 1 out of 6 randomly selected people had one or more parasites. Parasites have become pandemic for many reasons, including contaminated water supplies, day care centers, ease of international travel, foods, increased immigration, pets and the sexual revolution. Most people will meet a parasite at some point in their lives. Contrary to popular myths, having parasites isn't a reflection of cleanliness.

Common symptoms of parasites are abdominal pain, allergy, anemia, bloating, bloody stools, chronic fatigue, constipation, coughing, diarrhea, gas, granulomas, irritable bowel syndrome, itching, joint and muscle aches, ner-

vousness, pain, poor immune response, rashes, sleep distur-
bances, teeth grinding, unexplained fever and unexplained
weight loss.

Many physicians request parasitology testing on random
stool samples. This can be highly inaccurate, so repeated
testing is often necessary for definitive results. Since many
parasites live farther up the digestive tract, many labs now
give an oral laxative to induce diarrhea to detect these parasites. Others are found by using a rectal swab rather than a
stool sample. The most accurate stool testing is usually done
by labs that specialize in parasitology testing. You can order
a parasitology test along with a Comprehensive Stool Analysis for an additional modest fee. (See Resources in *Digestive
Wellness* for laboratories that provide tests.)

Case Study: Matty

When I first began working with Matty, she was 17 years old, and her parents
felt that she had an eating disorder. When I questioned her about her eating
habits, she informed me that she avoided all fat, that eating nearly anything
caused pain and that she needed to be very cautious about her foods. She
seemed, at first glance, stereotypical of a teenage girl trying to watch her
weight to fit into the fashion scene. Many teenage girls trying to live up to
societal standards have bizarre eating habits and patterns that can easily lead
to eating disorders.

I listened to Matty carefully. She told me that she needed to nap nearly
every day and that the fatigue would come upon her suddenly. For years
almost any time she ate or drank she had stomach pains about ten minutes
to an hour later. She felt gassy and bloated all the time and had daily headaches and difficulty concentrating. She had daily bowel movements, with some
constipation. While difficult, her menstrual cycles were then regular, although
until recently she often skipped cycles.

We began working on her digestion by giving her supplements of acidophilus, bifidobacteria and digestive enzymes. She also began eating every 2
to 3 hours. Although she experienced a nearly immediate improvement in
energy level, the bloating and many problems remained. Her physician or-
dered a Comprehensive Digestive Stool Analysis with parasitology and a candida antibody test. What appeared to be an eating disorder turned out to

be amoebic dysentery! A simple course of medication relieved her digestive problems, fatigue, limited eating style and headaches. Over time, other problems were resolved as well.

FOOD AND ENVIRONMENTAL SENSITIVITY TESTING

If you have food and/or chemical sensitivities, you probably have a leaky gut. In fact, Jean Munroe, M.D. states that 70 percent of her patients with multiple chemical sensitivities have leaky gut.[15] In order to heal an inflamed gut mucosa, it really helps if you can identify and avoid specific foods which increase the inflammation. Testing can help you pinpoint exactly which foods bother you. There are two main ways to test for food sensitivities: an elimination/provocation diet and blood tests. It's advisable to do both.

Elimination/Provocation Testing: The Elimination/Provocation Test is a low-allergy diet which allows you to feel changes in your body by first eliminating and then reintroducing foods you might be sensitive to. The foods allowed during the elimination test are unlikely to cause food sensitivities. Over the past few years, I have been using an elimination diet that works well for nearly all my clients, except those with candida, Crohn's disease and ulcerative colitis. This program allows you to eat rice, all fruit (except citrus), all vegetables (except tomatoes, eggplant, potatoes and peppers), fish and olive oil. White rice is more easily digested than brown rice and typically causes less sensitivity. You can eat as much of these foods as you like, plus you can use olive oil for stir-frying and salad dressings. You may want to combine this with a detoxification program (detailed below). People with candida can eliminate fruit and add poultry. People with Crohn's disease or ulcerative colitis can eliminate rice and add poultry.

If food sensitivities are provoking your symptoms, you will feel better when eating this way. In fact, some people feel better than they have in years! Eliminating the offending foods over several months' time gives your digestive system a chance to heal because you are no longer irritating it. During this time it's best to refrain from eating any foods which might aggravate your symptoms.

After 7 to 14 days of being on the elimination diet, you begin what's called the *provocation challenge*. By slowly reintroducing foods into your diet, you can test your reactions. Every two days add a new food. Eat the food at each meal. Try to eat the food in its original form. For example, eat cooked whole wheat, rather than wheat bread or pasta. Keep a record of how you feel, noting any symptoms. Do you become sleepy 30 minutes after eating wheat? Does cheese give you diarrhea? Do you itch all over after eating oranges? Do your joints ache after eating tomatoes? Do you react differently to organically grown foods? Through careful observation, you can detect many foods you have become sensitive to. It may be necessary to test a food several times to be certain of your reactions.

While the Elimination/Provocation Test sounds simple, administering it can be tricky. People generally have no problem with the elimination part; a restricted food plan can be accomplished for a week. Slowly adding foods back into your diet is more difficult. Eating simple foods is helpful when determining which foods you may be sensitive to, but most recipes and restaurant foods have many ingredients. Sometimes it's hard to determine which food caused the problem. You may feel badly after eating something, but not be certain which ingredient caused the distress. It then becomes necessary to remove all suspected foods for four days, and try them again one at a time. If you experience the same symptoms/reactions each time you add the food, you've found the culprit.

If you have food sensitivities to one food, you are often sensitive to all foods in the same family. For example, people who are sensitive to wheat are often sensitive to all grains in the grass family. It is common to be sensitive to more than one food or food family.

Be careful to avoid foods that you are sensitive to. Each

time you eat an offending food, it irritates the intestinal mucosa. Avoiding it allows the intestines to heal, and you will gradually stop reacting to most of the foods which originally bothered you.

Blood Tests for Food Allergies/Sensitivities: While many foods may be unmasked during the Elimination/Provocation Test, others may remain hidden. Blood tests which quantify antibody reactions are simple, effective ways to screen for food and environmental reactions. Look for a lab which tests for IgG or IgG4 antibodies. Some labs also include additional testing for IgA, IgE and/or IgM antibodies. Your doctor will receive a detailed readout which documents your personal reaction to a large variety of substances. Most laboratories also include a list of prepared foods which contain hidden sources of the offending foods, a rotation menu and other educational material to help you in the healing process.

Functional Liver Profile Testing: This test is useful for determining how well your liver can handle toxins. For this test you take a caffeine tablet, an asprin and two Tylenol. Each of these substances is detoxified by a specific liver pathway and converted into specific metabolic byproducts. Measurements from your urine of these metabolites can pinpoint how well your liver is handling the job and where it is failing.

GETTING WELL

If you have leaky gut syndrome and want to get well, a wealth of therapies can help you. A health professional can guide you through the options, but you have to do the work! The good news is that the steps you take to heal your gut will provide you with healthful habits for the rest of your life. Wouldn't you like to feel more vibrant and alive five years from now than you do today? Hopefully, you'll begin by making some changes in the way you approach living and healing.

Sidney Baker, M.D. talks about "tacks rules" in his lectures and in his new book, *Detoxification & Healing*.[16] The rules are (1) if you are sitting on a tack, it takes a lot of aspirin to make you feel good; (2) if you are sitting on two tacks, removing just one does not result in a 50 percent improvement. So in order to get better, you must discover how many tacks you are sitting on and carefully remove each and every one. Then you will feel a whole lot better. This may take quite a while.

Remember: You've been unwell for a long time, and it will take some time to become well again. Persistence and perseverance are two necessary ingredients in this plan. Remember to honor your unique needs. What works for someone else may work for you or make you ill. Just as each of us has a unique face and body, our biochemical needs vary dramatically, too.

RESTORING DIGESTIVE FUNCTION

Fortunately, there are many ways to heal your gut, based on your particular problem. Some involve changing your habits, like learning to chew your food more thoroughly; others involve taking specific supplements that will help your body repair itself.

Chew Your Food Carefully: Healthy digestion begins with chewing! We chew to increase the surface area of the food we eat so that our digestive system doesn't have to work so hard. Saliva contains digestive enzymes that begin the process of digesting carbohydrates and fat. The parotid glands under the tongue send messages to the brain and digestive tract to let them know what to expect. When we don't chew thoroughly, we miss all these healthful benefits.

Deal with Your Food Allergies: When you know you have a food allergy or sensitivity, the very best thing is to avoid those foods completely for 4 to 6 months. That may seem cruel, but if you really want your gut to heal, this is the best way. If you are sensitive to a wide variety of foods, a rotation diet may suit you. There are many fine books out about rotation diets, including *If It's Tuesday It Must Be Chicken.*

Treat Dysbiosis: Dysbiosis is treated according to the specific bacteria, fungi and/or parasites you have. Your physician will be able to give you a choice of prescription medications or natural remedies. The most effective natural substances are Berberine, capryllic acid, garlic, grapefruitseed extract, mathake tea, oil of oregano capsules, pau d'arco and tanalbit.

Candida fungi respond to a wide variety of natural substances and dietary changes. Eat a low carbohydrate diet, such as the zone diet, and avoid sugar, alcohol and vinegar.

When candida fungi are killed, the protein fragments and endotoxins released trigger an antibody response. This can initially produce a worsening of the person's symptoms and is commonly known as a *dieoff,* or a *Herxheimer, reaction.* Therefore, it is important to begin therapeutics gently, increasing small doses gradually. If your symptoms are still aggravated, cut back the supplements and then increase them again gradually. Most people begin to feel dramatically better within two weeks. If not, either you're not dealing with a candida problem, or it is part of a much larger picture. Ask your health professional to make therapeutic recommendations.

Because yeast's main function is to survive, some of the cells will. After you've been on a specific remedy for a month or so, switch to a different one. That will kill the ones that have become resistant. It's also advisable to rebalance your normal flora by taking a good probiotic supplement.

Replenish Intestinal Flora: Does it surprise you to know that there are more bacteria in your digestive system than cells in your body? Four pounds! These bacteria are of three main types: those that cause disease, those that have an apparently neutral effect (commensal) and those that actually benefit us (flora). The proper balance of these microbes is essential to the health of our digestive tract and total body.

Beneficial bacteria are called *intestinal flora, probiotics* or *eubiotics* (the last two terms mean "healthful to life"). The two most important groups of flora are the lactobacilli, found mainly in the small intestine, and bifido bacterium, found primarily in the colon. These bacteria live in a mutually beneficial relationship that has evolved to enhance our health and theirs. Mostly, they live in a harmonious symbiotic relationship with us. We offer them a warm, moist home with lots of food, and they, in turn, provide vitamins and other substances that lower our risk of disease and cancer, moderate the effect of drugs, determine the ecology and functioning of the intestines and affect our immune competence and rate of aging.

Flora play an important role in our ability to fight infectious diseases, providing a front line in our immune defense. They manufacture antibiotics, acids and hydrogen peroxide which make the intestinal environment hostile to competing microbes. Some flora have anticancer and antitumor properties. Friendly flora also manufacture many vitamins, including the B-complex vitamins biotin, thiamin (B1), riboflavin (B2), niacin (B3), panthothenic acid (B5), pyridoxine (B6), cobalamine (B12) and folic acid, plus vitamin A and vitamin K. Lactic acid-secreting acidophilus and bifidus increase the bioavailability of minerals which require acid for absorption: calcium, copper, iron, magnesium and manganese.

Take a mixed probiotic supplement that contains *at least* lactobacillus and bifidobacteria. Supplements that come refrigerated as powders or capsules usually have the highest potency.

Dosage: Take 1/4 to 1/2 teaspoon or 1 to 2 capsules 2 to 3 times daily. Start with small doses and gradually increase to avoid a dieoff reaction.

Case Study: Kyle
My son, Kyle, seemed like a normal newborn, but he developed an eczema rash when he was ten days old. Initially, we tried vinegar and water washes, Monostat cream and other home remedies for a yeast infection. After they were exhausted, a pediatric dermatologist prescribed a topical cream which the pharmacist custom-blended. Despite our energies, by the time Kyle was four months old we had tried every possible remedy except cortisone. He looked like he had been burned from his lower back around to his belly button. A holistic pediatrician suggested that we give him a flora preparation called *Bifidus infantus*, the intestinal flora found most commonly in infants. Within two weeks his rash was nearly gone, and in four weeks it was totally gone. We continued to give Kyle the flora every time he had even a small diaper rash or cradle cap.

Use Fructooligosaccharide (FOS): Over the past decade Japanese researchers have studied oligosaccharides, the most common of which is fructooligosaccharide (FOS). These sugar molecules rapidly increase the growth of food bifidobacteria and lactobacillus. Fructooligosaccharides are in many foods but are especially high in bananas and are also found in barley, fruit, garlic, Jerusalem artichoke, onions, soybeans and wheat. Supplemental FOS is usually made from soybeans. FOS does such a good job of restoring gut ecology that it is possible to regain health in many cases without the use of medication.

Take Digestive Enzymes: People with leaky gut syndrome usually have incomplete digestion. Use of digestive enzymes, either plant-based or pancreatic, can significantly reduce the bloating and gas caused by the fermentation of partially digested food. However, products differ. Some may contain ox bile, which helps with the emulsification of fat. Others may also contain hydrochloric acid to help with protein digestion in the stomach. Plant-based enzymes work at a large span of pH, whereas pancreatic enzymes only begin to work in the more alkaline small intestine. Plant enzymes, therefore, offer a broader effect. Pancreatic enzymes, on the other hand, may be more beneficial for diabetics or people with hypoglycemia because they stimulate repair and maintenance of the pancreas. If you are lactose intolerant, you may benefit from taking lactase enzymes with dairy foods.

Dosage: 1 to 2 with meals, 3 times daily or as needed.

Hydrochloric Acid May Help: As we age the parietal cells in the stomach produce less hydrochloric acid (HCl). In fact, half of all people over the age of 60 have hypochlorhydria (low stomach acid), and by age 85, 80 percent of the healthy people tested had low stomach acid.[3] Low HCl levels open us to the possibility of food poisoning, dysbiosis and bacterial overgrowth of the small intestine. Adequate HCl is critical for absorption of vitamin B12 from food. This vitamin deficiency causes weakness, fatigue and nervous system problems. Absorption of minerals in the duodenum also depends upon normal HCl levels. (A Heidleberg Capsule Test can be used to measure HCl levels.)

Dozens of conditions and symptoms signal low hydrochloric acid, including belching, bloating, constipation, diarrhea, food allergies, heartburn or gas immediately after meals, indigestion, nausea after taking supplements and chronic parasites and candida infections. (See *Digestive Wellness* for more details.)

Dosage: Begin with one 10 mg capsule of betaine HCl with each protein-containing meal. If you do not feel a warm sensation in your tummy, add an additional capsule at the following meal. You can build up to a total of 50 mg. If you feel a burning or warm sensation, you've taken a bit too much. If you are uncomfortable, you can neutralize the acid with a glass of milk, a teaspoon of baking soda in water or Alka-Seltzer Gold. Then, cut back to a comfortable level.

REDUCING OXIDATIVE DAMAGE WITH ANTIOXIDANTS

Cells in our bodies are continuously being damaged by molecules called *free radicals* or *reactive oxygen species (ROS)*. These highly reactive substances are produced in the body as a consequence of metabolism or from exposure to alcohol, cigarettes, drugs, radiation, rancid oils, stress, sun or other toxic substances. Free oxygen radicals (such as hydrogen peroxide, hydroxyl radical, lipid peroxide, singlet oxygen and superoxide) are unstable molecules looking for an electron, which they will grab from any available spot. The fatty acids in our cell membranes, mitochondrial membranes and nervous system are the primary targets. Free radicals can also damage DNA, which determines how our cells replicate, and enzymes, which direct cellular function. Once the intestinal tract has been damaged, free radicals are often produced in quantities too large for the body to process. This causes inflammation and irritation, which exacerbate a leaky gut. A single free radical can have a cascading effect, damaging up to one million cells. The potential for damage depends on your body's ability to recognize the situation and the availability of antioxidant nutrients.

Fortunately, our bodies and food sources have evolved so that we have multiple mechanisms to recognize and defuse free radicals. For example, to combat hydrogen peroxide, we have an enzyme called glutathione peroxidase, which contains vitamin E and selenium. To combat superoxide radicals, we have superoxide dismutase, which may contain copper, manganese or zinc. The most powerful antioxidant substances are bioflavonoids, carotenoids, coenzyme Q10, glutathione, lipoic acid, selenium and vitamins C and E. Melatonin, secreted by the pineal gland while we sleep, is also an important hormonal antioxidant. Glutathione, N-acetylcysteine and cysteine are potent antioxidants, which support the liver detoxification pathways to help minimize toxic overload in the body.

All the antioxidants work together as a team to protect us. Each has a specific job which complements the others so they must be used in balance. For example, once vitamin E has done its work, it gets changed into a tocopheroxyl radical and no longer works as an antioxidant. But vitamin C and glutathione can regenerate vitamin E so that it can work once more. Recent research has shown that folic acid also has antioxidant properties, helping repair DNA from free radical damage. It's my guess that eventually we'll find that nearly every nutrient plays a role in oxidative protection.

Fresh fruits and vegetables, nuts and seeds are loaded with antioxidants. Ginger and most of our kitchen spices also provide protection from reactive oxygen species. In fact, most foods in their natural state contain an abundance of these protective nutrients. Not surprisingly, processing foods uses up many of the antioxidants naturally found in them.

It's important to note that there has to be a correct balance between antioxidants and ROS. Taking more and more antioxidant supplements is not the answer, because although we mainly focus on the negative aspects of free radicals, they do have important physiological functions. They help us remove electrons from sugar and fat molecules so they can be burned for fuel. One way we kill invading bacteria and viruses is to bleach them to death with hydrogen peroxide. It's when they are not kept in proper balance that the trouble begins.

Dosage: Take a multivitamin or antioxidant supplement

which contains 200 mcg selenium, 400 to 800 IU vitamin E, 10,000 IU or more beta carotene and at least 500 mg vitamin C. It may also contain coenzyme Q10, cysteine, n-acetylcysteine, glutathione and lipoic acid, among other nutrients.

DETOXIFICATION: HOW TO REMOVE THE TOXINS

Over the past several years, I have personally and professionally relied on three main detoxification programs that are effective and gentle: fruit and vegetable cleansing, metabolic cleansing and vitamin C flushes between cleansings.

Fruit and Vegetable Cleansing: This is gentle but effective. You eat all you want of fruits, vegetables and rice and use olive and canola oils as condiments for 7 to 10 days. If you choose to continue after that time period, you can add fish, poultry, legumes, nuts and seeds. Fresh fruit and vegetable juices are an excellent source of easily assimilated nutrients and alkalizing minerals and can enhance detoxification pathways. It's important to eat every two to three hours to keep your blood sugar levels normal.

The major benefit of this detox method is that you can do this on your own without professional supervision. Of course, if you are under a doctor's care or taking medication of any kind, you'll need to let your physician know of your plans. The first few days may require some mental and physical adjustments to your new regimen, but most people feel a sense of general well-being. You may notice that many of your outstanding symptoms have disappeared or become less aggravated.

You may also experience some discomfort during the first three or four days. Headaches are fairly common and may be the result of withdrawal from alcohol, caffeine, sugar or other substances. They are an indicator that toxins are being flushed out or that your body is going through withdrawal. To facilitate this, drink a lot of water, diluted juices and all herbal teas except those containing caffeine. Some people develop rashes or pimples as the skin works hard to eliminate toxins. Taking saunas, steambathing and massaging your skin with a soft, dry brush or loofa can help. If you are constipated, toxins may be reabsorbed into your bloodstream, causing symptoms such as headaches and nausea. If constipated, take a fiber supplement; psyllium seeds or freshly ground flax seeds work well. Begin with 1 teaspoon in water, and drink up quickly before it turns into a gel. Aloe vera juice may also help regulate your bowels. And make sure you are eating enough fiber-rich fruits and vegetables.

Metabolic Cleansing: Though gentle, metabolic cleansing is a deep method of detoxification, and it is the best, most thorough program I have used. Its purpose is to allow your digestive system to rest, relax and heal itself. The foundation of the program is a hypoallergenic, rice-based protein and nutrient drink or detoxification supplement.[17] In addition to taking it, you eat high-fiber, low-allergy foods like rice, fruits, vegetables and olive oil.

During a metabolic cleanse most people experience a dramatic alleviation of their symptoms and a distinct improvement in their energy level. The high levels of nutrients found in the drink and in the fruits and vegetables help the liver activate its detoxification pathways and move unwanted materials out of the body.

Note that this program is administered only through health professionals who can monitor your progress, determine when you should quit and help you adjust if you have any difficulties.

Vitamin C Flush: The vitamin C flush can be used between metabolic cleansings or at the first sign of a cold or infection. High levels of vitamin C help detoxify the body, rebalance intestinal flora and strengthen the immune system. If your immune system is weak or you've been exposed to a lot of toxins, you may want to do a vitamin C flush once a week for a month or two.

To do a vitamin C flush, you must take vitamin C to the level of tissue saturation. You'll know you've reached it because you'll have watery diarrhea. You need to purchase powdered mineral ascorbate C, which is more easily tolerated by most people because it doesn't change your pH balance. The amount you take depends on your personal needs that day. Many of us require about 5,000 mg; others need 15 or 20 times as much. For instance, if you're coming down with a cold, have chronic fatigue syndrome or are under excessive stress, you may need 50 to 100 grams to induce a flush.

Instructions: Take two or three teaspoons of vitamin C powder, mix with water or fruit juice and drink. Half an hour later, repeat. If you don't have diarrhea 30 minutes after the second dose, do it again. If you haven't gotten diarrhea after three doses, take 2 to 3 teaspoons every 15 minutes. If you still haven't experienced diarrhea after another hour, increase the dosage. Stop once you get diarrhea. Keep track of how much vitamin C you take. This will help you determine your optimal dosage or how much vitamin C to take the next time you do a flush. Your optimal dosage is three-quarters of the amount it takes to produce a vitamin C flush.

REDUCING YOUR EXPOSURE TO TOXIC SUBSTANCES

Everybody's exposed to toxic substances every day that they can't control—exhaust fumes, second-hand cigarette smoke and air pollution. But there are other things you can control, including the following:

- Reduce your intake of medications, especially nonsteroidal pain medications and antibiotics.
- Use alcoholic beverages in moderation, if at all. Because of the good press that red wine has received recently, there has been an upswing in its use. Truly, grapes contain many beneficial phytonutrients, such as polyphenols and reservatrol, but the same benefits can be achieved by drinking organic grape juice. Alcohol is a toxic sub-

stance and puts a heavy burden on the liver and intestinal tract.

- Buy organic foods, whenever possible. The average person consumes one pound of herbicides and pesticides each year. Our bodies must work very hard to get rid of these substances. Because they are fat soluble, many get stored in our tissues.
- Reduce or eliminate food additives. The average person consumes about 14 pounds each year, including antimicrobials, colorings, emulsifiers, flavorings, humectants and preservatives.[18] They've been tested singly, but never in combination. What are the long-term effects? No one really knows, but certainly they increase the toxic load on our liver, kidneys and gut-activated lymphatic system. Read labels carefully and buy produce in a natural food store. You'll find many new foods and many convenience foods that are similar to the ones you love! Be brave!
- Research is linking pesticides to breast cancer. They really aren't good for us—not in our homes or on our food. Reconsider the use of herbicides and pesticides around your home and workplace. Find a comfortable balance between weeds and lawn. Take time to dig the weeds out, or pay neighborhood children a nickel for each dandelion root they pull! Make peace with the ants in your kitchen. They come inside to get out of the rain. Can you share your space with them?
- Use natural cleaning products and cosmetics. Natural cleaning products are much more user-friendly and do a terrific job. Read the list of ingredients on your shampoo or hand lotion. Do you really want that inside your body? What you put on your skin goes into your body.

RULES FOR A LIFETIME OF HEALTHFUL EATING

Your challenge is to find a way of eating and living that suits your emotional and physical needs. The word "diet" comes from Greek and means "a manner of living" or "way of life." The Latin root means "a day's journey." Choose a diet that works for your specific needs and lifestyle. The key is to make real changes you can live with successfully on a long-term basis. The following twelve rules provide important guidelines.

1. Eat Local Foods in Season: Local foods are fresh and have the highest levels of nutrients. They also have the largest energy fields and the greatest enzyme activity. Ask the produce manager at your supermarket to purchase locally grown products whenever possible. Make it part of your routine to shop at local farm stands and farmer's markets.

Eating foods in season also helps cut down on the amount of pesticides and herbicides we consume. Foods that are flown in from outside the country—grapes from Chile, coffee from South America, bananas from Mexico—are not regulated by the same pesticide standards as foods grown in the United States. Often we get back on imported produce the very pesticides that we banned here.

2. The Life in Foods Gives Us Life: Food is fuel. Food gives us energy. Because we really are what we eat, if we eat foods that have little enzyme activity, they don't spark our body to work correctly. Enzymes are to our body what spark plugs are to the engine of our car. Without those sparks, the car doesn't run right. If a food isn't biologically useful, who needs it?

3. Plan Ahead and Carry Food with You: If you carry a bag lunch, you know it'll be healthy because you made it at home where you have only healthy foods. Pack some leftovers or a quick sandwich with a salad and/or a piece of fruit. Special containers and Zip-Loc bags simplify the process. Planning meals ahead of time also helps you consolidate shopping trips and ultimately conserves time.

4. Eat Small, Frequent Meals to Sustain Energy Levels: Snacking is the best trick I know for boosting energy levels. People in Europe, South America and Japan stop in the middle of the afternoon to have tea. Our children rush home from school and eat us out of house and home. Only American adults are too busy to stop. If you find that from 3 to 6 PM it's difficult to concentrate, try this simple trick: Have something to eat in the middle of the afternoon and again just before you leave work.

A few quick snack ideas: Eat the half a sandwich you saved from lunch and a piece of fruit, a bagel and cream cheese with tomatoes, a rice cake with peanut butter and apples, a cup of soup and several pretzels or a handful of nuts and raisins. You'll find your energy level will stay more constant throughout the day.

5. Eat When You Are Hungry; Stop When You Are Satisfied: This sounds like a simple statement, but often we eat when we aren't hungry because we're angry, bored, depressed, lonely or because we're at a social event and everyone else is eating. Before you eat anything, ask yourself the simple question: Am I hungry? If you are, then eat. If you aren't, divert your attention to other activities.

6. Avoid High-Calorie, Low-Nutrient Foods: Make each bite count! Avoid high-sugar, high-fat, high-salt, low-fiber foods. Avoid all foods with restructured vegetable oils: hydrogenated, partially hydrogenated or vegetable shortenings. Limit your intake of nonnutritive foods to less than 10 percent of your total caloric intake, but allow for an occasional splurge! Remember: 90 percent for your body, 10 percent for your soul!

7. Choose Organically Grown Foods Whenever Possible: Organic foods generally have higher levels of nutrients because organic farmers pay more attention to their animals' health and to their soil. Animals raised on organic farms are given foods that nature intended. We benefit because we don't get extra doses of hormones and antibiotics added to our foods. Organic farmers add more nutrients to the soil because they know that healthy plants can better fend off pests and that those nutrients end up in the foods. Bob Smith of Doctor's Data has released a study which analyzed organic versus commercially grown apples, pears, potatoes, wheat and wheat berries. He found that mineral levels in organically grown foods were twice as high on average as commercially grown foods.[19]

8. Eat as Many Fruits and Vegetables as Possible: I can't stress enough the positive benefits of eating fruits and vegetables. The available research is overwhelming! They are chock full of vitamins, minerals, fiber and phytochemicals (plant chemicals) that protect us from cancer, heart disease and probably everything else. Research on phytochemicals is in its infancy, yet very promising. Citrus and other fruits, chives, garlic, green tea, grapes, onions, soybeans and other legumes, tomatoes and cabbage family foods, which include bok choy, broccoli, brussel sprouts, cauliflower, collards, kale, kohlrabi, mustard greens, rutabaga and turnips, all contain phytochemicals that protect us from developing degenerative diseases. It's best to eat at least five half-cup servings a day, but more is better—up to 9 or 11 servings daily.

9. Drink Clean Water: Unfortunately, many cities fail to provide excellent water. The sources are often groundwater that is easily contaminated by runoff. The EPA estimates that 1.5 trillion gallons of pollutants leak into the ground each year, with the highest incidence of contaminants from lead, nitrates (from fertilizers) and radon. Over 700 chemicals have been found in tap water, but testing is done on less than 200 of these.[20]

There isn't one correct answer about where to get the best drinking water. Various authorities argue the benefits of bottled, distilled, energized, filtered and reverse osmosis waters. If you have a well, have the water tested for bacterial content and pollutants. Find out about your local drinking water— where it originally comes from, how it's processed and if it has fluoride added to it. Ask your water department for an analysis. There is much controversy today about the use of fluoride and chlorine in tap water. The levels of chlorine needed to kill bacteria are rising due to increasing bacterial resistance, but chlorine has been strongly associated with elevated cancer risks.

10. Eat Lots of Fiber: Americans eat only about half as much fiber as is required for healthy digestive function and health. Most protein foods contain little or no fiber. When Dennis Burkitt, the father of the fiber revolution, first discovered fiber, he believed its value was only for roughage. Yet, now we know high-fiber diets also protect our colons; they reduce the incidence of polyps and bowel diseases and the risk of developing colon cancer. Soluble fiber binds to toxic substances for excretion from the body.

Fiber is the preferred food of the colon cells. Without it they cannot thrive and repair. One beneficial source of fiber is inulin, a substance found in asparagus, chicory, jerusalem artichoke flour and onions. The best source—25 to 40 g daily—is from your diet. Foods highest in fiber are fruits and vegetables, grains, legumes, nuts and seeds. You can supplement from 1 teaspoon to 2 tablespoons daily with barley bran, flaxseed meal, inulin, oat bran, psyllium seeds and wheat bran. People with food sensitivities need to select a type of fiber that does not provoke an allergic response.

11. Respect Your Own Biochemical Uniqueness: Remember the foods that are best for you are foods that agree with your body and your unique biochemistry. The rest of your family may have little or no problem eating wheat or dairy products, but if you do, it's best to avoid them. If you are invited to someone's home, call several days ahead of time to let the host know you are on a restricted eating program. If your host can't accommodate your needs, perhaps you can bring a dish that suits you or have a snack before you go and eat what you can. Restaurants are more used to accommodating people with specific dietary needs, so speak up.

12. Relax While Eating: Many times we don't even stop long enough to sit down when we eat. Yet eating is a time of rejuvenation of body and spirit. Take a few extra minutes to enjoy and relish the food that you eat. Take a few moments to reflect on your day and your life. Doing this can help keep your whole day in balance.

One way I've found to encourage peace of mind during meals is to say grace. It puts me in touch with the bounty of the earth we live on, makes me pay attention to the people I am with and be grateful for their presence in my life, helps me thank the people who produced the food and reminds me that we all depend upon each other and on community.

BETTER COPING SKILLS FOR STRESS MANAGEMENT

Prolonged stress changes the immune system's ability to respond quickly and affects our ability to heal. Guided imagery, meditation, relaxation and a good sense of humor can help us deal with daily stressors. It helps if we can learn to let small problems and traumas wash over us, not taking them too seriously. Learning to go with the flow can really help us live in a more healthy manner.

EXERCISE

Fitness isn't just a fad. It's not optional. It's one of the best all-around tools for healing. It reduces stress, helps prevent infection, aids the heart and circulation, helps build "good" HDL cholesterol and maintains blood sugar levels. If we want to be healthy and vibrant, we must find an activity that suits us and do it regularly.

Dosage: Do some type of exercise at least three times a week for at least 20 to 30 minutes. More is better, but don't overdo. You should feel invigorated after exercising, not like taking a nap.

REBUILDING INTESTINAL MUCOSA WITH SUPPORTIVE NUTRIENTS

Most nutrients help restore digestive integrity. A comprehensive program of nutritional supplements will help the cells regenerate, providing a ladder that helps us climb out of the deep hole we're in. Begin your program with a good multivitamin with minerals. You'll find the following nutrients (beginning with the most important) offer special benefits when healing a leaky gut. You can find them in products especially designed to enhance gut function.[21]

Glutamine: This is the most abundant free amino acid in the body and blood. Glutamine has two nitrogen groups which it shuttles from place to place as needed. It is an essential amino acid for rapidly dividing skin and mucus membrane cells throughout the body. The cells of the small intestine, white blood cells and macrophages use glutamine as their preferred food. When we are ill or the digestive tract is leaky, glutamine can help heal the intestinal lining more effectively than any other nutrient. A side benefit is that we feel stronger and our muscles get less fatigued.

Dosage: From 2 to 8 g daily.

Gamma-oryzanol: A compound found in rice bran oil, gamma-oryzanol is a useful therapeutic tool in treating gastritis, irritable bowel syndrome and ulcers. It has a healing effect throughout the digestive tract. It can normalize cholesterol and serum triglycerides, symptoms of menopause and depressive disorders.

Dosage: 100 mg three times daily for three weeks. May be used longer as needed.

Seacure: Seacure is a supplement made from deep ocean whitefish which has been broken down into peptides (short protein chains) and amino acids. The peptides have a restorative effect on gut function in leaky gut syndrome, Chrohn's disease, irritable bowel syndrome and other digestive problems.

Dosage: Six capsules daily in divided doses, best before meals.

Vitamin A: This is an essential nutrient for healthy eyes, mucous membranes and skin. Without adequate amounts of vitamin A, these tissues are unable to maintain themselves. Vitamin A itself can be toxic in levels above 8,000 IU daily. However, betacarotene is a precursor to vitamin A and provides a nontoxic source that can be converted as needed into vitamin A. Many plant foods are rich sources of carotenoids; all green, yellow and orange vegetables, particularly carrot juice and yams. Spirulina, blue-green algae and other "green" supplement foods are also loaded with carotenoids, plus enzymes and many trace nutrients. Diabetics and people with thyroid disorders may have difficulty converting carotenoids and may need to take preformed vitamin A.

Dosage: 8,000 IU. More is not necessarily better since vitamin A can be toxic in high dosages. However, a physician may prescribe higher doses.

Vitamin C: This vitamin has strong antioxidant properties and assists in the production of collagen for wound healing throughout the body and digestive system. Vitamin C can bind to viruses and toxic substances, pulling them out of the body. (See vitamin C flushes above.)

Dosage: From 1,000 to 10,000 mg daily, or the amount that is three-quarters of your bowel tolerance. Whatever dosage you take, be consistent.

Pantothenic Acid/Vitamin B5: This vitamin has many functions. Of benefit to the adrenals, panthothenic acid is used in the conversion of food to energy and in the synthesis of the neurotransmitter acetylcholine. Research has shown that panthothenic acid helps in the gut-healing process.

Deglycyrrhized Licorice: Licorice root has many health-enhancing properties. It is soothing to the mucus membranes of the digestive tract, and chewable licorice can help reduce inflammation and pain. It promotes healing of mucus membranes by stimulating production of prostaglandins that promote healing and cell proliferation. It also has antibiotic and antioxidant properties. Be sure to buy deglycyrrhized licorice; regular licorice root can raise blood pressure levels and lower potassium levels.

Dosage: Chew 2 tablets between meals as needed up to four times daily.

Folic Acid: Recent research has shown that folic acid also has antioxidant properties that help repair and protect DNA from free radical damage. It is especially important for the mucus membranes because of their rapid turnover.

Dosage: From 800 mcg daily. May be used therapeutically in doses up to 10 mg.

Milk Immunoglobulin Concentrates: Concentrated whey products contain high levels of protective secretory IgA. Concentrated whey products, such as Probioplex®, can help normalize dysbiosis and chronic diarrhea for many people. However, if you are dairy sensitive, you may have trouble with this product.

Dosage: Varies with product. Typical dosages: 1/2 teaspoon or 2 tablets three times daily between meals.

Schizandra: An old Chinese tonic, schizandra is sometimes called an adaptogen, because it is believed to normalize physiological functions. It has well-documented effects as a sedative and antioxidant, protects and repairs the liver and has been used successfully in people with hepatitis to stabilize liver function.[22]

Zinc: This is an essential nutrient for immune function and wound healing. It is found in every tissue of the body and in cell membranes, hormones and hundreds of enzymes. It is essential for healthy reproductive function.

Dosage: 15 to 50 mg zinc daily.

REFERENCES

1. "Intestinal Permeability Application Guide" (manual), Asheville, N.C.: Great Smokies Diagnostic Laboratory, 1996; J. Bland, M. Swanson, "Comprehensive Digestive Stool Analysis and Intestinal Permeability" (audiotape), Asheville, N.C.: Great Smokies Diagnostic Laboratory, 1995; E. Eggermont, "Gastrointestinal manifestations in cystic fibrosis," *Eur. J. Gastroentrerol. Hepatol.* 8(8): 731-38 (Aug. 1996); R.M. Van Elburg, "Intestinal permeability in exocrine pancreatic insufficiency due to cystic fibrosis or chronic pancreatitis," *Pediat. Res.* 39(6): 985-91 (June 1996); H.Z. Apperloo-Renkema, et al., "Host-microflora interaction in systemic lupus erythematosus (SLE): colonization resistance of the indigenous bacteria of the intestinal tract," *Epidemiol. Infect.* 112(2): 367-73 (Apr. 1994); A. Benard, et al., "Increased intestinal permeability in bronchial asthma," *J. Allergy Clin. Immunol.* 97(6): 1173-78 (June 1996); P. D'Eufemia, et al., "Abnormal intestinal permeability in children with autism," *Acta Paediat.* 85(9): 1078-79 (Sept. 1996); H. Mielants, et al., "The role of gut inflammation in the pathogenesis of spondyloarthropathies," *Acta Clin. Belg.* 51(5): 340-49 (1996).
2. *Ibid.*; "Do intestinal hyperpermeability and the related food antigens play a role in the progression of IgA nephropathy?," *Am. J. Nephrol.* 16: 500-05 (1996).
3. L. Galland, "Solving the Digestive Puzzle" (conference manual), Great Smokies Diagnostic Laboratory/HealthComm International Inc., San Francisco, May 1995, p. 10.
4. J. Bland, *20-Day Rejuvenation Diet,* New Canaan, Conn.: Keats Publishing, 1997; T. Thompson, "Approach to Gastrointestinal Immune Dysfunction and Related Health Problems" (lecture), 4th International Functional Medicine Meeting, Aspen, Col., 1997.
5. G. Spaeth, et al., "Food without fiber promotes bacterial translocation from the gut," *Surgery* 108(2): 240-47 (Aug. 1990).
6. G.M. Swank, E. A. Deitch, "Multiple organ failure: bacterial translocation and permeability changes," *World J. Surg.* 20(4): 411-17 (May 1996); M.P. Fink, "Effect of critical illness on microbial translocation and gastrointestinal mucosa permeability," *Semin. Respir. Infect.* 9(4): 256-60 (Dec. 1994); G. Spaeth, "Microbial translocation from the gastrointestinal tract: Pathophysiologic phenomenon or catalyst for multiple organ failure?" *Zentralbl. Chir.* 1994(4): 256-67.
7. T. Godwiala, et al., *Amer. Col. Gastroenterol.,* Oct. 18, 1988.
8. Adapted and used with permission from C. Resnick, Tyler Encapsulations, Gresham, Ore.
9. R. Jaffe, M.D., "Gut hyperpermeability," *Serammune Physicians Laboratory Newsletter* 2(1), Jan. 1992.
10. T. Mitsuoka, "Intestinal flora and aging," *Nutr. Revs.* 50(12): 438-46 (Dec. 1992).
11. A. Benard, et al., "Increased intestinal permeability in bronchial asthma," *J. Allergy Clin. Immunol.* 97(6): 1173-78 (June 1996).
12. *Ibid.*

13. "Guide to Health," Ft. Lauderdale, Fla.: Immuno Laboratories, Inc., 1994; R. Jaffe, M.D., educational brochure, Reston, Va.: Serammune Physicians Laboratories.
14. "Intestinal Permeability Application Guide" (manual), Asheville, N.C.: Great Smokies Diagnostic Laboratory, 1996.
15. J. Munroe, M.D., "Medical Causes and Treatment of Leaky Gut Syndrome" (audiotape), Asheville, N.C.: Great Smokies Diagnostic Laboratory.
16. S. Baker, M.D., *Detoxification & Healing*, New Canaan, Conn.: Keats Publishing, 1997.
17. Several companies make these products, including Biotics, Metagenics, Progressive Laboratories and Tyler Encapsulations.
18. "Ultrabalance" (workbook), Ceig Harbor, Wash.: HealthComm, Inc., 1988, p. 111.
19. B. Smith, "Organic foods vs. supermarket foods: element levels" (unpublished study), West Chicago, Ill.: Doctor's Data, 1993.
20. "Health Studies Collegium Information Handbook," Reston, Va.: Serammune Physicians Laboratories, 1992.
21. Many companies make these products, including Biotics, Metagenics, Progressive Laboratories and Tyler Encapsulations.
22. X. Li, "Bioactivity of neolignans from frutus Schizandrae," *Mem. Institute Oswaldo Cruz* 86 (2, Suppl.): 31-37 (1991).

RECOMMENDED READING

If you want to learn more about leaky gut syndrome, I encourage you to read my book, *Digestive Wellness* (Keats, 1996), which goes into the subject in greater detail. The following books are other excellent resources.

Jeffrey Bland. *20-Day Rejuvenation Diet*. New Canaan, Conn.: Keats Publishing, 1997.
William Crook. *The Yeast Connection*, 1985. *The Yeast Connection and the Woman*, 1995. Jackson, Tenn.: Professional Books.
Sherry Rogers. *Tired or Toxic*, 1991. *Wellness Against All Odds*, 1992. *The E.I. Syndrome: Environmental Illness*, 1995. Syracuse, N.Y.: Prestige Publishers.
Judy Shabert and Nancy Erlich. *The Ultimate Nutrient Glutamine*. Garden City Park, N.Y.: Avery Publishing, 1994
John Trowbridge and Morton Walker. *The Yeast Syndrome*. New York: Bantam Books, 1986.